Little Pebble™

What's In Th[e] ... e

raintree
a Capstone company — publishers for children

Raintree is an imprint of Capstone Global Library Limited, a company incorporated in England and Wales having its registered office at 7 Pilgrim Street, London, EC4V 6LB – Registered company number: 6695582

www.raintree.co.uk
myorders@raintree.co.uk

Edited by Erika L. Shores
Designed by Cynthia Della-Rovere
Picture research by Svetlana Zhurkin
Production by Katy LaVigne

ISBN 978 1 4747 0603 2 (hardcover)
19 18 17 16 15
10 9 8 7 6 5 4 3 2 1

ISBN 978 1 4747 0608 7 (paperback)
20 19 18 17 16
10 9 8 7 6 5 4 3 2 1

British Library Cataloguing in Publication Data
A full catalogue record for this book is available from the British Library.

Acknowledgements
Dreamstime: Eti Swinford, 7, Sonya Lunsford, 19; Getty Images: Gary John Norman, 5; Minden Pictures: Mark Moffett, 15; Shutterstock: Africa Studio, 1, artem_ka, back cover, 2—3, Christopher Elwell, 21, gorillaimages, 9 (left), Hector Ruiz Villar, 17, J. Helgason, 6 and throughout, Kitch Bain, 8 and throughout, KPG_Payless, 9 (right), Madlen, 4 and throughout, Miroslav Beneda, 13, Photo Fun, cover, 11

Every effort has been made to contact copyright holders of material reproduced in this book. Any omissions will be rectified in subsequent printings if notice is given to the publisher.

Printed in China.

Contents

Dig and peek!

Dig a hole.

Peek under ground!

What lives in the soil?

Plants

Roots hold plants in soil.

roots

We eat some roots.

Dig up carrots.

Look at these potatoes!

Animals

Squirm!

Worms tunnel in soil.

They eat dead plants

and soil.

11

Ants dig a nest.

Ants live together

in groups called colonies.

A tarantula hides.

Quick!

It grabs an insect

to eat.

Dig!

Moles tunnel.

Hairs on their nose

help them to feel.

This owl lives in
a burrow.
It catches food
with its claws.

Bark! A prairie dog warns others.
They stay safely in their burrows.

Soil makes a good home.

Glossary

burrow underground home

colony group of animals that lives together

prey animal that is eaten as food

root plant part that grows under
the soil and sucks up water

tunnel dig a passage through soil

Read more

Animals that Dig (Adapted to Survive), Angela Royston (Raintree, 2014)

Burrow (Look Inside a...), Richard and Louise Spilsbury (Raintree, 2013)

Rocks and Soil (Real Size Science), Rebecca Rissman (Raintree, 2013)

Websites

www.bbc.co.uk/gardening/gardening_with_children/didyouknow_worms.shtml
Find out more about worms.

www.bbc.co.uk/nature/life/Burrowing_Owl
Learn about the burrowing owl.

Index